1.99

WILD FLOWERS OF THE
CHANNEL ISLANDS

A Little Souvenir by Sue Daly
with Chris Andrews

CHRIS ANDREWS PUBLICATIONS LTD & GATEWAY PUBLISHING LTD, SARK

Bluebells and Sea
Campion, Herm

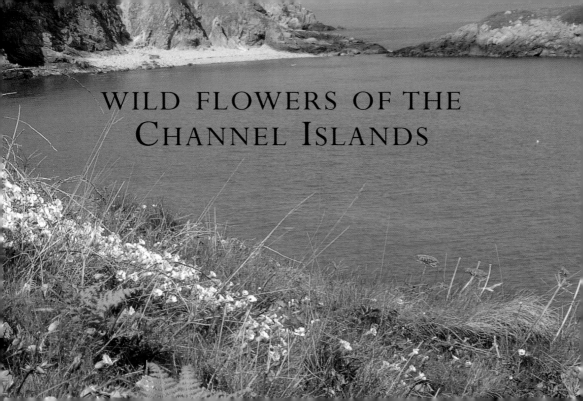

WILD FLOWERS OF THE
CHANNEL ISLANDS

Introduction

The wildflowers of the Channel Islands are a fascinating blend of the exotic and the common, the native and those that have been introduced. The Islands' southerly position and gentle climate allow species to thrive here that are rarely, if ever, found on the British mainland and there are even a few that live nowhere else in the world. Although covering just a few square miles, the Islands contain a rich variety of habitats from woodland, pasture and wet meadow inland to sandy heathland, dunes and cliffs on the coast. Each environment is home to its own mixture of wildflowers and, with so many different habitats, the list of plants recorded in the Islands is a long one. There are over fifteen hundred species in Jersey alone.

The mild climate also means that there is barely a month without wildflowers. A local saying tells of how kissing is out of fashion when Gorse is not in bloom, a reference to the fact that the prickly bush flowers just about all year. It is at its most fragrant in late winter when the banks and hedgerows are brightened by Snowdrops and the first Daffodils. These are quickly joined by swathes of Dog Violets, Primroses, Three-cornered Leek and Bluebells. As spring warms to summer wildflowers paint the Channel Islands all the colours of the rainbow on a lush green canvas framed by the turquoise sea. By late summer the brighter colours have faded making way for the gentle purples of Autumn Squill, Bell Heather and Wild Thyme.

Daffodils in St Peter's, Guernsey

6   Rock Astor and Mesembryanthemums with Fort Homeaux Florians, Alderney

Many wildflowers have evolved to survive in only a very specific environment and quickly perish if their surroundings change. The tiny Sand Crocus and Wild Pansy, for example, are dependant on the rabbits that graze the sandy areas where they grow. If the rabbits disappear the larger plants they keep at bay by their constant nibbling quickly take over, smothering the smaller plants beneath them. Wet meadows are home to several species of orchid as well as many of the islands' other floral treasures. Boggy fields however are not the most productive for farmers yet the simple act of draining them is fatal to the plants who need such damp places. The greatest threat of all comes from the total destruction of the countryside to make way for buildings and tarmac. As the human population of Guernsey and Jersey continue to grow, so does the pressure on the countryside of these, the two largest Islands. The smaller Islands face less of these problems and conservation groups and government departments in all of the Islands strive to protect the most valuable wild places. Their hard work means that the wildflowers of the Channel Islands will continue to amaze and delight all who visit these beautiful Islands and those lucky enough to live here.

Three-cornered Leek and Hoary Stock, Alderney

CLIFFS & ROCKY SHORES

The cliffs and rocky shores of the Channel Islands would appear to be the least hospitable environment for wildflowers. Autumn and winter gales drench the granite heights and send salt-laden spray far inland. In summer the sun and wind combine to dry everything to a crisp. Yet many wildflowers have evolved to live in this turbulent realm between land and sea. Most have extremely long roots to hold them in place and seek out the traces of water and many have thick, leathery leaves to retain their precious moisture. From early spring onwards these toughest members of the plant world put on a stunning natural display that outshines many gardens.

Rocquaine Bay, Guernsey and Wild Cabbage

12　Bluebells above Maseline Harbour, Sark

Gorse, Havre Gosselin, Sark

Common Broomrape

Bell Heather, Sark

16   Birdsfoot Trefoil

Scarlet Pimpernel

18 Prostrate Broom

Samphire

Sea Campion

Tree Mallow

Thrift or Sea Pinks

Yellow Horned-poppy

Sheepsbit Scabious

Many of the beaches in the Channel Islands are restrained by a seawall but where the coast has been left to itself the landscape reveals every stage in a wonderful biological succession from bare sand to dune and heathland. The wildflowers closest to the sea stabilize the sand and often have thick, fleshy leaves to protect them from the extremes of heat and salinity. Further inland many more lime-loving plants stake their claim nourished by the crushed remains of seashells and rotting seaweed blown up from the beach. Beyond the reach of the sea yet more wildflowers carpet the heathland with colour and scent the air with their fragrance through the warmer months of the year.

Wild Thyme

DUNES & HEATHLAND

Spotted Rock-rose

Yuccas and the dunes at St Ouen's Bay Jersey

26 Autumn Squill

Alderney Sea-lavender

Burnett Rose

Dwarf Pansy

Hare's-tail Grass

Green-winged Orchid

Evening Primrose

30   Lizard Orchid

Bee and Viper's Bugloss on Herm

Pyramidal Orchid

32   Red Campion & Hogweed

Rosy Garlic

Sand Crocus

34 Burnet Rose

Sea Holly

36   Bell Heather on Guernsey

Wild Leek, Bracken and Shell Beach Herm

Les Blanches Banques, Jersey

The mild climate and few severe frosts mean that discarded garden plants which would perish just a little further north survive wild in the Channel Islands. Some have literally found their own niche among the local flora, such as the Ivy-leaved Toadflax and St Peter Port Daisy which thrive on the Islands' granite walls. Others have made more of an impact on native wildflowers such as the Hottentot Fig which forms dense, heavy carpets on the cliffs. It spreads rapidly, smothering less vigorous plants and often its sheer weight brings down whole sections of rock and soil.

Hottentot Fig (above)
Mesembryanthemums (opposite)

FLORAL INVADERS

42   Ivy-leaved Toadflax

Tree Lupin

St Peter Port Daisy

Wet Meadows

Many wet meadows and patches of marshland have been drained in the Channel Islands and much of this precious wildlife habitat has been lost. However, some wet meadows in Jersey and Guernsey are protected and it is the orchids that attract the most human attention. The Loose-flowered or Jersey Orchid is generally the tallest and is a continental species not found in the wild on the British mainland. The three lower-growing species of orchid are difficult to tell apart, a task made all the more confusing by the hybrids that have developed. Naming each bloom, perhaps, is of lesser importance, for a swathe of mixed orchids set against the lush green background of a water meadow is one of the most striking sights in the Channel Islands.

Marsh Orchids and Yellow Bartista

Loose-flowered Orchids

Purple Loosestrife

Spotted orchids

50   Ragged Robin   Self-heal

Yellow Iris

WOODLAND, BANK & HEDGEROW

The network of lanes and tracks that criss-cross the interiors of the Channel Islands are bordered with hedgerows, banks and walls which provide valuable natural habitat for all kinds of wildflowers. The woodlands harbour yet more floral treasures, often nestling in sheltered valleys protected from the worst of the desiccating maritime wind. A walk along a quiet country lane or dappled woodland path offers a refreshing change from more bracing elements of the coast and is just as rewarding for those with a passion for wildflowers.

Bluebells in Dixcart Valley, Sark

54 Common Dog Violet,   Alderney Geranium

Blackthorn

Common Ramping Fumitory

Giant Butterbur

Germander Speedwell

58 Hawkweed

Honeysuckle

60   Milkwort

Red Campion

Primrose

62 Catchfly

Common Toadflax

Three-cornered Leek

Wall Pennywort

Produced by Chris Andrews Publications Ltd with Gateway Publishing Ltd, Sark

Tel: +44(0)1865 723404 **www: cap-ox.co.uk**

ISBN 978 1 905385 94 2

Photographed by Sue Daly with Chris Andrews. Design: Mike Brain. Text: Sue Daly.

Front Cover: Gorse above La Maseline, Sark

Back Cover: Poppies

Title Page: Scarlet Pimpernel